THE SLOW COOKING GUIDE

Modern recipes for
slow cooking all year round

THE

Slow

Cooking

GUIDE

NH
NEW
HOLLAND

First published in 2019 by New Holland Publishers
London • Sydney • Auckland

Bentinck House, 3–8 Bolsover Street, London W1W 6AB, UK
1/66 Gibbes Street, Chatswood, NSW 2067, Australia
5/39 Woodside Ave, Northcote, Auckland 0627, New Zealand

newhollandpublishers.com

A record of this book is held at the British Library and the National Library
of Australia.

ISBN 9781760791186

Group Managing Director: Fiona Schultz
Publisher: Fiona Schultz
Editor: Elise James
Designer: Yolanda La Gorcé
Production Director: Arlene Gippert
Printer: Toppan Leefung Printing Limited

10 9 8 7 6 5 4 3 2 1

Keep up with New Holland Publishers on Facebook
facebook.com/NewHollandPublishers

CONTENTS

INTRODUCTION

All foods, as we know, are prone to seasonal change. This is because our food histories and cultural eating practices usually originate from the land, from the simple beginnings of subsistence farming and peasant cookery. There is, however, another kind of food seasonality – different foods come in and out of favor according to the fashions of the time.

What was in fashion 10 years ago is different from what is in vogue today. The fascinating part of the current change in food perceptions is the return of many of the old ways of cooking. Fast food has definitely been put in its place and a return to slow food is very much back in the public's perception of what is both good for you and what is presentable at the table. Within the idea that some of the old ways of cooking are truly worthy and should be enjoyed alongside quick meals, speedy salads and wok-tossed minute meals, there is a strong place for the slow and hearty reside foods of old.

The slow cooking pot that bubbled away for hours on the edge of the fireplace made a successful electronic conversion in the late 60s and early 70s and became the 'crockpot'.

Like most fashions, crockpots were heartily embraced and people realized that an appliance that could slow-cook a wet meal automatically (usually without the need for stirring or watching over) was a convenient way to produce wonderful traditional family meals without being tied to the kitchen for the entire day. The crockpot has, however, like many food innovations become identified with the time of its invention and is now seen as old technology. Ask your mum and she probably still has one stashed in the back of her cupboard somewhere or under the preserving equipment gathering dust in the back shed. It will likely be beige or burnt orange in color with a motif on the side – a testament to the time of its previous popularity.

These cookers have recently had a makeover and with the resurgence of interest in slow food and traditional cooking techniques they are perfectly placed to again be seen with pride bubbling away on the side of the kitchen bench, imparting beautiful aromas to your kitchen while happily cooking, unaided and unsupervised.

Traditional slow-cooked soups, continental casseroles, hearty stews and exotic tagines – the traditional and slow foods from all nations – are back on the food agenda and the poetic and provincial idea of slow cooking inexpensive cuts of meat is seen at some of the nest eateries around the Western world. In short, the slow cooker is back, looking good and ready for service in the modern kitchen.

Once you have started cooking with a slow cooker you will soon realize its convenience and economy. The slow cooker is a low-fuss appliance that is also a low-energy user – once the cooker reaches core temperature the mass of the food helps to retain its own heat and very little extra heat is needed to maintain temperature. Flavors are trapped inside the cooking environment and each component imparts its character and takes on the flavors of what is around it. Good quality stocks, fresh vegetables, citrus rinds and robust flavors such as rosemary and thyme are the winning elements to beautiful old-fashioned cookery.

One of the labor- and time-saving elements of this style of cooking is the fact that you can create the ultimate cooking short cut by cutting up your meats and vegetables and adding them to the one pot (your slow cooker) – the only things to wash are your cutting board and knife. The rest is taken care of from cooking to serving, leaving you with only the ceramic insert and the dinner plates for the after-dinner wash-up. There are few simpler and more fundamental ways of cooking.

GETTING TO KNOW YOUR SLOW COOKER

The various makes of slow cookers respond a little differently to each other so you'll need to gauge cooking time for yourself from the first couple of recipes you try out – if your cooker is particularly large or lower powered then you may need to add a little extra cooking time than the recipe indicates.

For the first few recipes mark down your starting and finishing time so that you quickly get a feel for how your particular slow cooker responds. Keep an eye on your slow cooker in the late stages of cooking to see if it requires any more or less cooking time or a top-up of liquid.

Your slow cooker is exactly that and cannot recover heat losses quickly, so lift the lid only when instructed. If you feel you must remove the lid several times, remember to extend the cooking time a little. You will learn whether to add extra time by simply looking at your meal in the late stages of cooking.

Due to the unique wraparound heating system, low temperature and long cooking periods, slow cooker temperatures cannot be accurately compared to an oven or a frying pan (see conversions on page 21). Cooking settings on most slow cookers are LOW and HIGH. Food will be broughtto simmer on all settings. The LOW and HIGH settings determine the time needed to reach a simmer. Avoid sudden temperature changes when using your slow cooker as it will not be able to withstand them. Do not put in frozen or very cold foods if the ceramic bowl has been preheated or is hot to the touch.

The removable ceramic bowl may be used in the oven and is ideal to use when adding a pastry crust to your favorite stews. Be careful not to place the ceramic bowl on the range surface or burners.

Your slow cooker can help you get the best advantage from your freezer. You can prepare double the usual quantity of a favorite casserole and when cooked, freeze the extra amount. The best way to freeze food for later reheating is to turn it out from the slow cooker after cooking to allow the ceramic insert to cool. Then wash the ceramic insert and coat it with a little oil or butter before returning the cooled food to it. Cover the ceramic insert and freeze until the food is set. Once set, turn out the block of frozen food and transfer it to a large freezer bag. Then when you return the food to the slow cooker for reheating, it will always fit back in perfectly. Do not use the ceramic bowl for storing food in the freezer indefinitely, and always remember that you cannot return frozen foods to a preheated cooker. When you want a slow-cooked meal without any preparation at all, just place the frozen food into the cooker and heat for 5 to 8 hours. The slow, gentle heating from the cooker will not dry out the meal you are reheating.You can prepare a recipe the night before in the removable ceramic bowl

and store it in the refrigerator so that when you are ready to cook the bowl can be transferred to the slow cooker heating base unit. Just make sure that the base unit has not been preheated. Cook on the desired setting for a little more time than given in the recipe.

Most vegetables should be cut into small pieces, or at least quartered, and placed near the sides and bottom of your cooker. Carrots and other dense root vegetables should be peeled and put where they will be covered by liquid.

An unusual characteristic of the slow cooker is that meats generally cook faster than most root vegetables. The heating element of the slow cooker runs around the outer edges of the insert and because of this it is a good idea to arrange vegetables towards that area.

Small food portions can be cooked in the slow cooker, but the times will vary. Because there is no direct heat at the bottom always fill the cooker at least half full to conform to the recommended times. Adjust your recipe volume according to the size of your slow cooker.

Roasts can be cooked on low without adding water, but a small amount of water is recommended because the gravies are especially tasty and it would be a shame to leave them behind.

The more fat or marbling the meat has, the less liquid you will need as the natural fats in the food help to baste and moisten the finished food.

Since the liquid content of meats and vegetables will vary, you may end up with a recipe with too much liquid. The excess can be reduced by removing the cover and setting the cooker on high for about 45 minutes.

Most recipes cooked in the slow cooker will be juicier since the slow cooking prevents evaporation. Your slow cooker should never be filled higher than 2 cm (3/4 in) from the top. If it is too full the lid will lift while the food is cooking.

With the high setting, if by chance your dish of food does dry out, do not simply add cold liquid; it is best to boil the kettle and add some extra water, or if you have extra stock, heat it in a small saucepan before adding to the slow cooker.

It is advisable to generally always preheat your slow cooker for 10 to 15 minutes before use. This helps food come up to cooking temperature faster.

ADAPTING YOUR FAVORITE RECIPES FOR THE SLOW COOKER

Here are a few basic hints that will help when you come to adapt other recipes.

- Allow sufficient cooking time on low setting.

- Follow the conversion guide given on the next page.

- Do not add as much water as conventional recipes indicate.

Always cook with the cover on. Your slow cooker cooks best if left undisturbed. Lifting the lid can lengthen the cooking time; if you need to stir your dish, do it during the last few hours of cooking time or only when instructed in the recipe.

Generally, 250 to 500 ml (1/2 to 1 pint) of liquid is enough for any recipe unless it contains rice, pasta or other absorbing grains such as polenta, couscous or quinoa. The other exceptions are pot roast-style dishes where you expect to have liquids at the end and classic Italian styled 'bolito-misto' dishes where you boil and simmer meats and discard the cooking liquid at the end of the cooking process. In the case of the pot roast, any vegetables and the main joint of meat can be lifted out at the end of its cooking time with a slotted spoon and tongs. Then, with the addition of thirsty grains such as those mentioned above, thick and wet rustic-style gruels can be made to form a magnificent base for a truly old-fashioned meal – simply turn the cooker to high, add some grains and cook for 45 minutes with the lid removed (while the main meat is rested and carved).

Slow cooking is one-step cooking – many steps in conventional recipes may be deleted. You can add all ingredients to the slow cooker at one time and cook for approximately 8 hours.

There are three important exceptions: milk, sour cream and fresh cream should be added during the last half hour of cooking.

When cooking with herbs and spices, whole herbs and spices are preferable. When a recipe calls for dried beans, the beans should be soaked overnight, then cooked on high for 2 to 3 hours. Or you can cook them overnight on low with water and 1 small teaspoon of bicarbonate of soda (baking soda) added to speed up the breakdown of the beans. Instead of soaking or cooking overnight, they may also be parboiled first. When a crisp topping of crumbs or grated cheese is called for, transfer food from the slow cooker to a platter and brown it either with a torch or in the oven. The removable bowls with some models are versatile, as they can be easily put in the oven to achieve the desired topping.

If cooked rice is called for, stir raw rice in with other ingredients. Add 250 ml (8 oz) of extra liquid per cup of raw rice. Use long-grain rice for best results in all-day cooking.

CLEANING AND CARING FOR YOUR SLOW COOKER

Never submerge the slow cooker cooking unit in water.

Remove the ceramic bowl and place the bowl in the dishwasher or wash with hot soapy water as soon as possible after emptying it.

Do not pour in cold water if the ceramic bowl is hot.

When cleaning your slow cooker do not use abrasive cleaning compounds.

A cloth, sponge or rubber spatula will usually remove the residue.

If necessary, a plastic cleaning pad may be used.

To remove water spots and other stains, use a non-abrasive cleaner or vinegar.

The metal liner may be cleaned with a damp cloth or scouring pad, or sprayed lightly with an all-purpose cleaner to maintain.

The outside of the slow cooker may be cleaned with soft

cloth and warm soapy water and wiped dry.

Do not use abrasive cleaners on the outside.

Care should be taken to avoid hitting the ceramic pot with metal spoons or water taps.

Do not put frozen or very cold foods in the slow cooker if the unit has been preheated or is hot to the touch.

Read all instructions and become thoroughly familiar with your slow cooker.

Do not touch hot surfaces; always use handles or knobs.

Caution must be used when moving the slow cooker if it contains hot oil or other hot liquids.

Close supervision is necessary when the slow cooker is used by or near children.

Unplug the slow cooker from the power outlet when not in use, before putting on or taking off parts, and before cleaning.

Use your slow cooker on an even and stable surface.

Do not place slow cooker units on or near a hot gas or electric burner, or in a heated oven.

Only the ceramic inserts should be placed in the oven or under a grill.

Converting traditional recipes for the slow cooker

With the guidelines in this introduction you should be able to take any appropriate recipe and convert it to a slow cooking recipe.

Think outside the square and make the slow cooker work

for you. Anything from a hearty porridge with dried fruit slowly cooked overnight to feed a family when it rises for a chilly winter breakfast or preparing a late sweet snack that cooks away as you settle in front of the television after the evening meal – the applications and variations are virtually unlimited.

COOKING TIME CONVERSION GUIDE

OVEN OR STOVE TOP	SLOW COOKER	SLOW COOKER
Cooking time	Low cooking time	High cooking time
15–30 mins	4–6 hrs	1½–2½ hrs
35–45 mins	6–8 hrs	3–4 hrs
50 mins–3 hrs	8–12 hrs	4–6 hrs

This guide applies particularly to casseroles. Most meat and vegetable combinations will require at least 7 hours on low.

All cookers consume approximately the same amount of power. The settings vary according to the make and size and individual style of each cooker, so if you are buying a new cooker, choose wisely and consider your potential end needs.

You can buy cookers with ceramic containers permanently fixed into the outer casings, where the heating elements are placed between the outer casing and the cooking pot. Some of these styles come with detachable power cords so that the entire unit can be taken to the table to serve from.

Another style of cooker has a removable inner ceramic cooking container, which means that only the cooking pot is taken to the table. This style of slow cooker enables food to be easily browned or crisped under the grill for final presentation. In these cookers the heating elements are fitted within the walls of the base unit that the ceramic container fits into.

There are different capacity cookers that vary from 1.5 to 5.5 liters (3 to 11 pints). While the little cookers seem kind of nifty and compact, it is best to get the largest size that you think you can use – once you become familiar with this appliance you will see the benefit of cooking double quantities and large joints of meat. It allows for greater versatility and is an easy way to feed a large number of guests.

BASICS, TIPS AND TRICKS

Cooking without liquid: You can cook without liquid. For example, fish and sausages can be placed in the cooker, covered, and cooked for 2 to 4 hours, depending on the thickness of the meat.

Rice: If cooked rice is called for, stir raw rice in with other ingredients. Add 250 ml (8 oz) of extra liquid per cup of raw rice. Use long-grain rice for best results in all-day cooking.

Dried Beans: When a recipe calls for dried beans, the beans should be soaked overnight, then cooked on high for 2 to 3 hours. Or you can cook them overnight on low with water and 1 small teaspoon of bicarbonate of soda (baking soda) added to speed up the breakdown of the beans. Instead of soaking or cooking overnight, they may also be parboiled first.

Toppings: When a crisp topping of crumbs or grated cheese is called for, transfer food from the slow cooker to a platter and brown it either with a torch or in the oven. The removable bowls with some models are versatile, as they can be easily put in the oven to achieve the desired topping.

Gravy: Remove the foods from the pot, leaving the juices. Prepare a smooth paste of about 60 g (2 oz) plain flour or corn flour to 60 ml (2 oz) water. Pour mixture into the liquid in your cooker and stir well. Turn to high and cook, stirring occasionally, until mixture thickens and becomes slightly transparent (approximately 15 to 20 minutes). Then it is ready to serve.

Foods to avoid:

- Crisp-cooked green vegetables

- Noodles

- Macaroni

- Asian vegetables

- Puddings or sauces made with a foundation of milk or cream.

SOUPS AND SIDES

CHICKEN VOL-AU-VENTS

1 1/2 kg (3 lb) roasting chicken
2 chicken stock cubes, crumbled
salt and freshly ground black pepper
1 bouquet garni
3 white onions, sliced
30 g (1 oz) butter
Approx 30 g (1 oz) plain (all-purpose) flour
250 ml (8 oz) cups milk
2 tablespoons dry sherry
45 ml (1 1/2 fl oz) Dijon mustard
1 red capsicum (bell pepper), finely chopped
340 g (12 oz) canned mushrooms, drained
4 spring onions (scallions), chopped
4 medium-size vol-au-vent cases
fresh parsley, chopped

Place chicken, stock cubes, salt and pepper, bouquet garni and onions in slow cooker. Cover with cold water and cook on low for approximately 4–6 hours or on high for 3–4 hours.

When chicken is cooked, allow to cool and cut flesh into small cubes. Strain stock, reserve 1 1/4 cups for the sauce and retain the rest for soups.

Heat the butter in a saucepan over low heat, add 4 teaspoons of flour and stir for a minute or two. Combine milk and reserved chicken stock and gradually stir into flour and butter mixture, whisking constantly. Bring to the boil, then reduce heat and add sherry and mustard. Stir until thickened. Gently fold in cubed chicken, capsicum, mushrooms and spring onions (scallions).

Pour sauce mixture into the empty slow cooker and keep hot on high. Meanwhile, bake vol-au-vent cases in the oven according to packet directions. To serve, spoon chicken mixture into pastry cases and garnish with chopped parsley.

TURKEY PATE

1 kg (2 lb) frozen turkey hindquarter
3 chicken stock cubes, crumbled
1 onion, sliced
1 stalk celery with leaves, sliced
1 carrot, roughly diced
salt and freshly ground black pepper
handful chopped liverwurst sausage
1 teaspoon dried thyme
4 spring onions (scallions), finely chopped
handful parsley, chopped
125 ml (4 oz) thin cream
45 ml (1 1/2 fl oz) coleslaw dressing

Thaw turkey hindquarter and remove as much fat and skin as possible, then place into slow cooker with stock cubes, onion, celery, carrot and salt and pepper to taste. Cook on low for approximately 5–6 hours or on high for 4–5 hours. Test for tenderness. When cooked, remove turkey, carefully wipe off any residual fat and allow to cool. Remove as much turkey meat as possible from the bones, then dice.

Using a food processor or blender, combine diced turkey meat, liverwurst, thyme, onions, parsley and a little of the cream.

Combine remaining cream with dressing and pour in, blending until quite smooth. Add salt and pepper to taste.

Serve in small pots, accompanied by very lightly buttered wholemeal bread.

COUNTRY STYLE PATE

500 g (1.1 lb) lean pork, minced
2 rashers bacon, finely diced
1 egg
45 ml (1 1/2 fl oz) sour cream
1/4 onion, minced
45 ml (1 1/2 fl oz) brandy
4 teaspoons plain (all purpose) flour
2 cloves garlic, minced
grated zest of 1/2 lemon
1/2 teaspoon salt
1/2 teaspoon freshly ground black pepper
1/4 teaspoon ground allspice
1/4 teaspoon dried thyme

Mix together pork, bacon, egg, sour cream, onion, brandy, flour, garlic, lemon zest, salt, pepper, allspice and thyme.

Oil a 500 g (1 lb) coffee can. Spoon meat mixture into the can and pat down. Cover with aluminium foil.

Place a trivet in the bottom of the slow cooker and place can on trivet. Cover and cook on high for 2 hours, or until firm. Allow to cool, then chill in the refrigerator.

CHICKEN CREPES

1 1/2 kg (3 lb) roasting chicken
2 chicken stock cubes, crumbled
1 onion, chopped
3 sprigs parsley
1 sprig thyme
120 g (4 oz) butter
1 spring onion (scallion), finely chopped
600 g (21 oz) button mushrooms, sliced
30 g (1 oz) plain (all-purpose) flour
salt and freshly ground black pepper
375 ml (12 oz) milk
20 ml (2/3 fl oz) dry sherry
45 ml (1 1/2 fl oz) thickened cream
3 hard-boiled eggs, chopped

Crêpe batter
240 g (8 oz) plain (all-purpose) flour
pinch of salt
2 eggs, beaten
20 ml (2/3 oz) olive oil
500 ml (1 pint) milk

Place chicken in slow cooker, add stock cubes, onion and herbs and cover with water. Cook on low for 4–5 hours or high for 3–4 hours. Remove chicken and chop flesh finely, discarding skin and bones. Reserve 120 ml (4 fl oz) stock. Melt butter in frying pan and sauté spring onion and mushrooms until softened but not brown. Blend in flour, season and cook for 1 minute.

Combine the milk and reserved stock and add to the pan gradually, stirring. Add sherry and cream, then cook gently until stock thickens. Adjust seasoning if necessary and fold through cooked chicken and hard-boiled eggs. Keep mixture warm in slow cooker on high, with lid slightly ajar.

To make batter, sift the flour and salt together and make a well in the centre. Add the eggs, oil, and half of the milk. Beat gradually drawing in flour from the sides. Slowly add remaining milk and 90 ml (3 fl oz) water, making a thin batter. Cover and set aside for at least an hour. Heat a little butter in a heavy-based 15 cm (6 in) frying pan. Add a little batter and tilt pan so that batter spreads evenly. When cooked on one side, turn and cook other side. Pile crêpes in a tea towel and keep warm.

Preheat the oven to 180°C (360°F). Place a spoonful of chicken sauce onto each crêpe, roll up and place into a greased ovenproof dish. Spoon over some of the sauce and bake for about 10 minutes. Serve remainder of sauce in a small jug at the table.

SPINACH AND PORK TERRINE

300 g (10 oz) frozen chopped spinach
375 g (13 oz) lean minced pork
1 egg
45 ml (1 1/2 fl oz) brandy
20 g (2/3 oz) fresh parsley, chopped
1/4 onion, finely minced
1/2 teaspoon salt
1/2 teaspoon dried thyme
1/2 teaspoon dried basil
1/4 teaspoon ground nutmeg
1/4 teaspoon freshly ground black
pepper
45 g (1 1/2 oz) chopped olives
4 rashers bacon
60 g (2 oz) ham, sliced
1 bay leaf

Thaw spinach and squeeze dry. Place pork, egg, brandy,
parsley and onion in a mixing bowl. Combine salt, thyme,
basil, nutmeg and pepper. Add half of seasoning mixture to
meat and mix well. Mix remaining seasoning mixture with
spinach and olives.

Line bottom and sides of a 10 x 18 cm (4 x 7 in) loaf pan (or
pan that fits in your slow cooker) with bacon. Spread with
one-third of the meat mixture. Cover with half the spinach
and half the ham slices. Top with another third of the meat
mixture and remaining spinach, ham and then finally with the
remaining meat mixture. Place bay leaf on top.

Cover with aluminium foil. Place a trivet in the bottom of the
slow cooker and place loaf pan on trivet. Cook in the slow
cooker on high for 2 hours. Chill, then slice to serve.

INDIVIDUAL VEGETABLE CREAMS

30 g (1 oz) butter
45 g (1 1/2 oz) white onion, finely chopped
250 g (8 oz) zucchini (courgette), grated
salt and freshly ground black pepper
60 g (2 oz) Parmesan cheese, grated
60 g (2 oz) Cheddar cheese, grated
90 ml (3 fl oz) thickened cream
2 large eggs, beaten

Heat butter in a frying pan and sauté onions for 10–15 minutes until tender and just beginning to brown.

Tip zucchini into clean absorbent paper and squeeze dry. Increase the heat in the pan, add the zucchini and toss for 5 minutes or so. Cover pan and cook for several minutes longer over low heat, until zucchini is tender. Season to taste and pour into a bowl.

Add cheese to the bowl, pour in cream and stir well. Fold eggs into mixture, then taste and adjust seasoning if necessary. (The mixture may be refrigerated at this stage until ready to cook. If you do this, allow a longer cooking time.)

Grease 4 small ramekins and pour custard into each. Put dishes into slow cooker, and pour enough water into the base of the cooker to come approximately halfway up the sides of the dishes. Cook on low for 1 hour with lid ajar.

Cook, covered, for another 3 hours, testing for firmness at the end of that time.

Test for firmness by inserting a knife blade into one of the custards – the blade should come out clean.

CHICKEN AND LEEK SOUP WITH HERB DUMPLINGS

4 chicken cutlets

1 onion, chopped

1 carrot, chopped

herb bundle made up of fresh tarragon, parsley and a bay leaf

1 1/2 L (3 pints) cups hot water

60 g (2 oz) butter

300 g (10 1/2 oz) potatoes, peeled, diced

3 large leeks, sliced

salt and freshly ground black pepper

2 boneless skinless chicken breasts, cut into small pieces

2 teaspoons chopped fresh tarragon

150 ml (5 fl oz) light cream

Dumplings

125 g (4 oz) all-purpose (plain) flour

1/2 teaspoon bicarbonate of soda

30 g (1 oz) fresh white breadcrumbs

50 g (1 3/4 oz) butter

handful of chopped fresh herbs, such as tarragon, parsley or chives

salt and freshly ground black pepper

75 ml (2 1/2 fl oz) water

Place the chicken, onion, carrot and bundle of herbs in a slow cooker with the hot water. Cover and cook for 2 hours on high, then strain the stock and skim off any fat. Finely chop the chicken, discarding the skin and bones.

Heat half of the butter in a large saucepan, add the potatoes and two-thirds of the leeks, cover and cook for 10 minutes. Transfer to the slow cooker and add 1 L (2 pints) of the stock and season. Cook for 50 minutes, until vegetables have softened. Blend in a food processor or with a hand-held blender until smooth, return to the slow cooker, then stir in the cooked chicken.

Make the dumplings while finishing the soup. Mix together the flour, bicarbonate of soda, breadcrumbs, butter, herbs and seasoning. Stir in water, then shape into 12 dumplings. Cook in simmering salted water for 15 minutes.

Add the rest of the butter and the chicken breast and the remaining leek. Cook for 2 hours, adding more stock if necessary. Remove from the heat and stir in the fresh tarragon and cream. To serve, divide between 6 bowls, drain the dumplings and add 2 to each bowl.

PUMPKIN SOUP

1 kg (2.2 lb) pumpkin, peeled, diced
400 ml (13 oz) canned tomato juice
4 teaspoons raw sugar
2 L (4 pints) water
salt and freshly ground black pepper
1 bay leaf
few drops of Tabasco sauce
2 chicken stock cubes
125 ml (4 oz) pouring cream
chopped fresh parsley, to garnish

With the exception of parsley and cream, combine all ingredients in a slow cooker and cook for 6 1/2 hours on low.

Remove bay leaf. Process the mixture a cupful at a time in a food processor.

Return mixture to slow cooker and reheat for 15 minutes. Add cream and allow to warm through.

Serve sprinkled with fresh parsley.

PORCINI MUSHROOM SOUP

Small handful dried porcini mushrooms

125 ml (4 oz) boiling water

45 ml (1 1/2 fl oz) olive oil

2 cloves garlic, crushed

1 leek, sliced

6 French shallots, chopped

285 g (9 oz) white mushrooms, thinly sliced

500 g (17 1/2 oz) forest mushrooms, including shiitake, oyster and Swiss brown, thinly sliced

15 g (1/2 oz) plain (all purpose) flour

1 L (2 pints) good quality chicken, beef or vegetable stock

250 ml (8 oz) double cream

1/2 bunch fresh flat-leaf parsley, chopped

30 fresh basil leaves, shredded

4 teaspoons fresh oregano

salt and freshly ground black pepper

ground nutmeg

Add the dried porcini mushrooms to the boiling water and set aside. When the mushrooms have softened, remove them from the liquid and set aside. Strain the mushroom liquid through a muslin-lined sieve to separate sand and grit, and reserve the liquid.

Heat the olive oil in a large saucepan and add the garlic, leeks and shallots and cook for about 3 minutes. Add the fresh mushrooms and cook over a very high heat until the mushrooms soften and their liquid evaporates (about 7 minutes). Reserve a few mushroom pieces for the garnish.

Transfer the leek and mushroom mixture to a preheated slow cooker set on high, then sprinkle with the flour and stir well to enable the flour to be absorbed. Add the stock and the

porcini mushrooms together with the reserved liquid. Stir to combine. Cook for 2 hours.

Add the cream, then turn to low and cook for a further 30 minutes or until slightly thickened. Add half the parsley and the basil and oregano and season to taste with salt and freshly ground black pepper. To serve, ladle into individual bowls sprinkle with extra parsley, reserved mushrooms, some nutmeg and a small dollop of extra cream if desired.

SPICED POTATO AND ONION SOUP

20 ml (2/3 fl oz) vegetable oil
1 onion, finely chopped
1 cm (1/2 in) piece fresh ginger, peeled, finely diced
2 large potatoes, cut into 1 cm pieces
2 teaspoons ground cumin
2 teaspoons ground coriander (cilantro)
1/2 teaspoon ground turmeric
1 teaspoon ground cinnamon
45 ml (1 1/2 fl oz) cold water
1 L (2 pints) chicken stock
salt and freshly ground black pepper
natural yoghurt to garnish

Heat the oil in a large saucepan. Cook onion and ginger for 5 minutes or until softened. Add the potatoes and cook for another 5 minutes, stirring often.

Mix the cumin, coriander, turmeric and cinnamon with cold water to make a paste. Add to the onion and potatoes and fry for 2 minutes, stirring well to release flavors.

Transfer the potato and spice mixture to a heated slow cooker set on a high setting. Add the stock and season to taste. Bring to the simmer and cover, then cook for 3 hours or until the potato is tender. Blend until smooth in a food processor or with a hand-held blender. Return to the slow cooker and heat through, then adjusting the seasoning again. Before serving garnish with the yoghurt and more pepper.

Serve with warm naan bread and salad.

SEAFOOD CHOWDER

500 g (18 oz) fish fillets (bream, snapper or cod)
125 g (4 oz) bacon, diced
1 medium onion, chopped
4 medium potatoes, peeled and cubed
1 teaspoon salt, or to taste
1/4 teaspoon freshly ground black pepper
375 ml (12 oz) evaporated milk

Cut fish into bite-size pieces. In a heavy-based frypan, sauté bacon and onion until meat is cooked and onion is golden.

Drain and put into slow cooker with the fish pieces. Add potatoes, 2 cups of water, salt and pepper.

Cover and cook on low for 5–8 hours. Add evaporated milk during last hour.

◊ NOTE: Chowder is a stew or thickened soup. It can be served as a meal on it's own or as a starter. It is especially good when mopped up with crusty bread.

CLASSICS

SALMON POACHED IN WINE

1 kg (2.2 lb) salmon fillet
250 ml (8 fl oz oz) white wine
1 bay leaf
1 sprig parsley
1/4 teaspoon salt
freshly ground black pepper
juice and grated zest of 1 lemon

Brush the inside of the slow cooker with olive oil. Rinse the
salmon fillet and dry with absorbent paper. Place the fillet
in the bottom of the slow cooker. Add the wine, bay leaf,
parsley, salt, pepper, lemon juice and zest.

Cover and cook on low for 3–4 hours. Serve either hot or
cold. This dish is delicious cold with a salad and crispy bread
and butter.

BEST-EVER MEATBALLS

2 teaspoons olive oil
1 medium onion, finely chopped
500 g (approx. 1 lb) lean beef mince
500 g (approx. 1 lb) minced turkey meat
salt and freshly ground black pepper
teaspoon dried tarragon
1/4 teaspoon dried basil
20 g (2 oz) plain flour
60 ml (2 fl oz) tomato paste
180 ml (6 fl oz) beef stock
2 teaspoons Worcestershire sauce
2 teaspoons apple cider vinegar
250 g (8 oz) mushrooms, sliced
250 ml (8 oz) sour cream

Heat 1 teaspoon olive oil in a large heavy-based frypan.
Sauté onion until golden and transfer to the slow cooker.

Shape meat into bite-size balls. Drop into frypan and sauté,
shaking to turn, until browned. Sprinkle with salt, pepper,
tarragon, basil and flour. Cook for a few minutes, then
transfer to slow cooker.

Add tomato paste, beef stock, Worcestershire sauce and
vinegar to frying pan. Stir to deglaze pan. Pour into slow
cooker, cover and cook on high for 1 1/2–2 hours.

Sauté mushrooms in remaining olive oil. Add to slow cooker
along with sour cream. Heat thoroughly, then serve with
French bread.

LASAGNE

45 ml (1 1/2 fl oz) olive oil
500 ml (1 pint) water
250 g (8 oz) minced beef
1/2 teaspoon salt
250 g (8 oz) lean pork, minced
1/2 teaspoon freshly ground black pepper
1 onion, finely chopped
250 g (8 oz) lasagne sheets
1 clove garlic, finely chopped
30 g (1 oz) mozzarella cheese, sliced thinly
1 teaspoon parsley, chopped
250 g (8 oz) ricotta cheese, crumbed
250 g (8 oz) tomato paste
Romano cheese, grated
1 1/2 teaspoon salt

Heat oil in a large saucepan, add beef and pork and brown with onion, garlic and parsley.

Stir in tomato paste, water, 1/2 teaspoon salt, and pepper and simmer, uncovered, for 1 1/2 hours.

Preheat oven to 180°C (350°F). Bring a large pot of water to the boil, add the salt and lasagne sheets. Boil for 20 minutes or until al dente, stirring constantly but very gently to prevent lasagne sheets from sticking together. Drain and set aside.

Wipe a little oil over the base of a large shallow rectangular baking dish, and arrange alternate layers of lasagne sheets, meat sauce, mozzarella and ricotta cheese. Repeat layers until lasagne sheets and sauce and two cheeses are all used, ending with ricotta cheese.

Sprinkle with grated Romano cheese and bake in the oven for 25–30 minutes. Allow to stand for 10 minutes before serving.

CHILI BEEF TACOS

2 teaspoons vegetable oil
500 g (1 lb) minced beef
2 onions, chopped
60 g (2 oz) taco seasoning mix
1/2 teaspoon freshly ground black pepper
45 ml (1 1/2 fl oz) tomato paste
125 ml (4 oz) beef stock
6 taco shells or corn tortillas

Heat the oil in a frying pan, and sauté the beef until browned. Add onion and cook until slightly softened. Stir in taco mix, pepper and tomato paste and cook for 1–2 minutes. Add stock and stir.

Transfer mixture to slow cooker and cook for approximately 4 hours on low. If mixture is too wet at the end of the cooking time, remove the cooker lid and cook on high until liquid has reduced.

Spoon beef mixture into heated taco shells or tortillas and serve at once with bowls of chopped tomatoes, cucumber and lettuce.

CONTINENTAL MEATBALLS

500 g (approx. 1 lb) minced pork
500 g (approx. 1 lb) minced veal
1 sachet onion soup
2 eggs
45 g (1 1/2 oz) quick-cooking rolled oats
250 ml (8 oz) milk
1/4 cup fresh parsley, chopped
salt and freshly ground black pepper
2 beef stock cubes, crumbled
1/4 teaspoon ground nutmeg
1/4 teaspoon ground allspice
125 ml (4 oz) beef stock

Preheat oven to 210°C (425°F). Place minced meats, onion soup, eggs, rolled oats, milk, parsley, salt, pepper, beef stock cubes, nutmeg and allspice in a mixing bowl. Mix until blended, then shape into 3 cm (1.2 in) balls.

Place 25 mm (1 in) apart in a shallow baking dish. Bake for 15 minutes or until browned.

Transfer to the slow cooker, pour in stock and cover. Cook on low for 1–2 hours.

Serve with sour cream or yoghurt.

PULLED PORK SLIDERS

250 ml (8 oz) barbecue sauce
125 ml (4 oz) apple cider
125 ml (4 oz) beef stock
1 tablespoon Worcestershire sauce
1 large onion, diced
2 cloves garlic, crushed
1 teaspoon thyme
1 teaspoon chili powder
2 kg (4 1/2 lb) pork shoulder
20–24 slider buns
Coleslaw, to serve

Combine all the ingredients except for the pork, buns and coleslaw in a bowl and stir. Pour half the sauce into a slow cooker, add the pork, then cover with the rest of the sauce.

Cook, covered, on high heat for 5–6 hours or on low heat for 10 hours. Remove the meat from the slow cooker and pour the sauce into a small saucepan. Bring the sauce to the boil and reduce it until it thickens.

Meanwhile, remove the bone from the pork and, using two forks, shred the meat. Put the meat and the thickened sauce back in the slow cooker to keep warm.

Slice the buns lengthwise, leaving a join at the back. To assemble the rollers, spoon in enough pork and sauce to fill it.

KEDGEREE

500 g (18 oz) smoked trout or cod
30 g (1 oz) butter
1 onion, finely sliced
1 teaspoon curry powder
200 g (7 oz) basmati rice
1 leek, diced, washed
500 ml (1 pint) boiling water
1 sachet Japanese dashi stock
30 ml (1 oz) cream
2 hard-boiled eggs, coarsely chopped
freshly ground black pepper
handful chopped fresh parsley

Place smoked fish in a saucepan, cover with cold water and bring slowly to the simmer. Cook for 6 minutes, drain and flake.

Melt butter in a large frypan over a medium heat and fry onion until soft. Add curry powder and cook, stirring, for 2 minutes. Add rice and leeks and fry gently for 5 minutes, stirring, until rice is translucent yet slightly brown in color.

Place rice mixture in a slow cooker and add boiling water, dashi stock and flaked fish. Gently stir to combine all ingredients, cover and cook on high for 2 hours.

When ready to serve add cream and eggs and toss gently with a fork. Season to taste with freshly ground black pepper. Sprinkle with parsley. Serve with lemon wedges if desired.

STUFFED VINE LEAVES IN TOMATO SAUCE

12 grape vine leaves, canned or fresh
400 g (14 oz) cooked brown rice
1 teaspoon dried mixed herbs
pinch of nutmeg
salt and freshly ground black pepper
1 teaspoon dried garlic
2 tomatoes, chopped and peeled
handful of parsley, chopped
2 spring onions (scallions), chopped finely

Tomato sauce

15 g (1/2 oz) butter
1 onion, diced
400 g (14 oz) canned Roma tomatoes, drained and chopped
2 teaspoons brown sugar
pinch of dried herbs
15 g (1/2 oz) tomato paste
50 ml (1 1/2 oz) dry red wine
handful parsley, chopped

If you are using fresh vine leaves, remove the stems, pour boiling water over leaves and leave for 1–2 minutes until softened. Dry, and lightly wipe over each leaf with a drop of oil. Combine all other ingredients to make the filling. Squeeze a handful of filling to make it firm and place onto leaf, then fold into neat little parcel, sealing with a little squeeze. Repeat with remaining leaves. Arrange carefully in base of slow cooker.

To make the tomato sauce, heat the butter in a frying pan and cook the onion until golden brown. Add all other ingredients and cook until blended. Spoon sauce into slow cooker over vine leaf parcels, and cook on high for approximately 1 1/2 hours or on low for 2–2 1/2 hours.

HERBED CANNELLONI WITH TOMATO SAUCE

250 g (8 oz) cottage cheese
30 g (1 oz) Parmesan cheese, grated
1 teaspoon mixed dried herbs
6 spring onions (scallions), finely chopped
salt and freshly ground black pepper
few drops Angostura bitters (optional)
8 instant cannelloni tubes

Tomato sauce

250 ml (8 oz) tomato purée
3–4 spring onions (scallions), chopped
2 teaspoons Worcestershire sauce
4 drops Angostura bitters
1 large clove garlic, crushed

Bring a large saucepan of salted water to the boil, add the pasta tubes and cook for 8 minutes or until just firm in the centre (al dente). Drain, set aside and keep warm. Place the cheeses, herbs, spring onions, salt and pepper and bitters in a bowl and mix thoroughly.

To make the sauce, mix together all ingredients. Lightly butter the base of the slow cooker. Spoon cheese mixture into cannelloni tubes. Spoon a little tomato sauce into the cooker, then arrange the stuffed cannelloni tubes in the cooker and spoon over remainder of sauce. Cook for 1–1 1/2 hours on high or 2–2 1/2 hours on low. Serve sprinkled with extra Parmesan cheese and parsley sprigs.

SLOW CHICKEN WITH RICOTTA, GREENS AND RED PEPPERS

(7 oz) fresh ricotta cheese

60 g (2 oz) chopped arugula (rocket)

45 g (1 1/2 oz) toasted pine nuts

100 g (3 1/2 oz) chargrilled marinated capsicum (bell pepper), chopped

salt and freshly ground black pepper

4 chicken breasts, skin on; each 170 g (6 oz)

20 g (2/3 oz) butter

240 ml (8 fl oz) chicken stock

Combine the ricotta, rocket, pine nuts, bell pepper and salt and pepper in a small bowl and mix together until smooth. Place 1–2 tablespoons of ricotta mixture under the skin of each chicken breast.

Place the chicken breasts in a slow cooker set on high, sprinkle with more salt and pepper, place 1 teaspoon of butter on each breast and pour the stock around the chicken. Cook for 2 hours on high. Serve the chicken with juices and a rocket salad.

ROASTS

SLOW ROAST CHICKEN

1 whole chicken, about 1 1/4 kg (2 1/2 lb)
1 sachet of French onion soup
2 red onions, cut into chunks
2 cloves garlic, sliced
125 ml (4 fl oz) white wine

Wash the chicken and pat dry. Sprinkle the French onion soup mix over the chicken and rub in.

Scatter the onions and garlic over the bottom of the slow cooker and place the chicken on top.

Cover and cook on low for 6–8 hours.

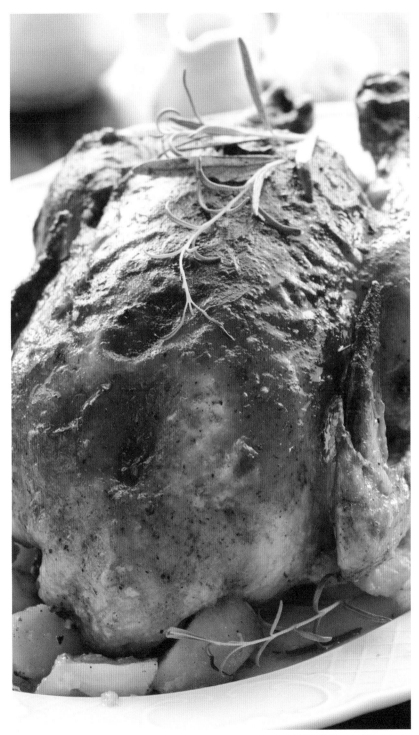

LAMB ROAST

45 ml (1 1/2 fl oz) tomato pasta sauce
20 ml (2/3 fl oz) fruit chutney
1 teaspoon curry powder
6 cloves garlic, crushed
1 leg of lamb
45 ml (1 1/2 fl oz) olive oil

Mix pasta sauce, chutney, curry powder and garlic together and set aside.

In a heavy-based frypan, brown the lamb in the olive oil. Place lamb in the slow cooker and pour the tomato mixture over the lamb. Cover and cook on low for 6–7 hours or on high for 4–5 hours.

Serve with roast vegetables.

POT ROAST

2 kg (4.4 lb) chuck steak roast
20 ml (2/3 fl oz) olive oil
4 cloves garlic, minced
250 ml (8 oz) dry sherry
90 ml (3 oz) soy sauce
1 1/2 teaspoons ground ginger
freshly ground black pepper
2 spring onions (scallions), thinly sliced
4 whole cloves

Rub roast with oil and minced garlic. Place meat in a glass
or ceramic bowl. Add sherry, soy sauce, ginger, pepper,
spring onions and cloves. Turn meat to coat. Cover and
refrigerate overnight.

To cook, remove meat from marinade and set marinade
aside. Transfer meat to the slow cooker. Add 120 ml (4 fl oz)
of the reserved marinade. Cover and cook on low for 7–8
hours, or until tender.

Transfer to a platter and keep warm. Add 120 ml (4 fl oz)
more marinade to pan juices. Cook down until reduced and
pour into a sauce boat. Serve sauce with meat.

SLOW BAKED PORK

1 kg (2.2 lb) boned shoulder of pork, rind removed
45 ml (1 1/2 fl oz) olive oil
2 teaspoons dried thyme
2 teaspoons dried oregano
1 teaspoon dried rosemary
4 cloves garlic, sliced
zest of 1 lemon
250 ml (8 oz) chicken stock
salt and freshly ground black pepper

In a heavy-based frypan, brown the pork on all sides in the
olive oil, then remove to the slow cooker. Place the herbs in
the slow cooker, then add the lemon zest.

Add the chicken stock and salt and pepper to taste. Cook
on low for around 8–9 hours and the meat will come apart
easily.

GLAZED HAM

2 1/2 kg (5.5 lb) boneless ham
3 tablespoons orange marmalade
1 tablespoon Dijon mustard

Trim fat from ham. Mix together marmalade and mustard and
spread on top of ham. Place in the slow cooker.

Cover and cook on low for 6–8 hours. Transfer ham to a
carving board. Pour meat juices into a sauce boat, skim off
fat and serve sauce with the ham.

GINGERED ROAST PORK

3 lb 5 oz (1.5 kg) pork loin or leg, well trimmed, tied with kitchen string
salt and freshly ground black pepper
3 Granny Smith apples, peeled, cored, quartered
15 g (1/2 oz) brown sugar
2 teaspoons ground ginger
1 teaspoon salt
10 g (1/3 oz) corn flour
20 ml (2/3 fl oz) water

Rub pork rind with salt and pepper. Arrange apples in base of slow cooker. Place pork on top of apples.

Combine brown sugar, ginger and salt. Spoon over top surface of pork. Cover and cook on low for 7 hours.

Ten minutes before serving strain off 240 ml (8 fl oz) of liquid into a small saucepan. Blend corn flour with water to make a smooth paste and stir into liquid. Heat until thickened. Remove string from the pork roll and carve. Serve with sauce, accompanied by the apples and freshly steamed vegetables.

STEWS, BRAISES AND CASSEROLES

CREAMY CHICKEN CASSEROLE

1 1/2 kg (3.3 lb) chicken thigh fillets, cubed
30 g (1 oz) plain flour
salt and freshly ground black pepper
1 onion, chopped
4 rashers bacon, chopped
125 g (4 oz) mushrooms, chopped
45 g (1 1/2 oz) butter
400 ml (13 oz) canned mushroom soup
250 ml (8 oz) water
60 ml (2 fl oz) thickened cream
fresh parsley, chopped

Coat chicken pieces with flour and season with salt and pepper. In a heavy-based frypan, sauté onion, bacon and mushrooms in the butter. Place chicken in the slow cooker, add bacon mixture and pour in soup and water (add more water if the sauce is too thick). Stir well.

Cover and cook on low for about 6 hours. Before serving, stir in cream and garnish with parsley.

CITRUS CHICKEN

1 lemon
1 1/2 kg (3 lb) roasting chicken
1 bouquet garni
3 carrots, thinly sliced
6 onions, thinly sliced
125 ml (4 fl oz) chicken stock
salt and freshly ground black pepper
pinch of nutmeg

Cream sauce
125 ml (4 fl oz) thin cream
175 g (6 oz) button mushrooms, sliced

Halve the lemon, squeeze out the juice and brush it all over the chicken. Place lemon skins in the chicken cavity. Lightly grease the slow cooker and add the bouquet garni. Place the chicken on top and arrange the carrot and onion around the outside. Pour around the stock, season to taste, add nutmeg, then cook for approximately 6 hours on low or 4–5 hours on high (cooking time will vary depending on the tenderness of the chicken).

To make the sauce, saute the mushrooms. Remove about 1/2 cup of chicken stock from the slow cooker, skim off as much fat as possible, and bring to the boil in a small saucepan. Add the stock and reduce, then add the cream and reduce to make a pouring sauce.

Serve chicken with the cream sauce.

LAMB HOTPOT

8 forequarter, neck or chump lamb chops, trimmed of fat
6 carrots, peeled and thinly sliced
6 parsnips, peeled and thinly sliced
6 onions, peeled and thinly sliced
6 potatoes, peeled, parboiled and sliced
salt and freshly ground black pepper
fresh parsley, chopped

Layer all ingredients except parsley in the slow cooker, ending with a layer of potatoes. Cover with water and cook on low for 8 hours or overnight, until lamb is falling off bones. Skim off any fat.

To serve, ladle out the meat and vegetables, spoon over the flavorsome juices and sprinkle with parsley.

This dish is wonderful with crusty bread to mop up the juices.

BURGUNDY CHICKEN CASSEROLE

8 skinless chicken thigh fillets
salt and freshly ground black pepper, to taste
1 onion, sliced
100 g (3 1/2 oz) brown mushrooms, sliced
1 red capsicum (bell pepper), sliced
1 sachet tomato/tomato and onion soup
375 ml (12 oz) chicken stock
250 ml (8 oz) red wine
1 tablespoon tomato paste
1 teaspoon Worcestershire sauce
1 teaspoon dried thyme

Place chicken in slow cooker. Season and cover with onion, mushroom and red capsicum. Combine remaining ingredients and pour over chicken and vegetables.

Cover and cook for about 6–7 hours on low. Remove chicken and stir sauce before serving.

HERB AND GARLIC LAMB SHANKS

4 meaty lamb shanks
2 cloves garlic, crushed
4 teaspoons dijon mustard
45 ml (1 1/2 fl oz) olive oil
750 ml (1 1/2 pints) chicken stock
2 teaspoons dried rosemary
2 teaspoons dried Italian herbs
salt and freshly ground black pepper

Score the outside of the lamb shanks and rub crushed garlic and Dijon mustard into them.

In a heavy-based frypan, heat the olive oil and brown the lamb shanks.

Place the browned lamb in the slow cooker, then pour in the chicken stock and sprinkle the herbs over the lamb. Add salt and freshly ground black pepper to taste.

Cook on low for 8–9 hours or 4–5 hours on high.

BEEF EN DAUBE

2 rashers bacon, diced
1 kg (2.2 lb) lean stewing beef, cut into 25 mm (1 in) cubes
2 cloves garlic, minced
24 small pickling onions
45 ml (1 1/2) olive oil
20 ml (2/3 fl oz) red wine vinegar
4 teaspoons brown sugar, firmly packed
375 ml (12 oz) dry red wine
salt and freshly ground black pepper
1/2 teaspoon dried thyme
250 ml (8 oz) beef stock
2 strips orange zest
8 teaspoons corn flour
fresh parsley, chopped

In a large heavy-based frypan, sauté bacon until crisp.
Remove from frypan and set aside.

Brown meat, garlic and onions in olive oil and transfer to the
slow cooker with bacon.

Add vinegar and brown sugar to frypan. Cook for 1 minute,
stirring. Pour in wine and bring to the boil, season and pour
over the meat. Then add the dried thyme, stock and orange
zest to the slow cooker. Cook on low for 8 hours.

Turn slow cooker to high. When bubbling, mix corn flour
with 45 ml (1 1/2 fl oz) water and stir in. Cook, stirring, until
thickened. Garnish with parsley and serve.

SWEET AND SOUR PORK

1 kg (2.2 lb) pork, cubed
1 onion, finely chopped
2 cloves garlic, crushed
1 red capsicum (bell pepper), sliced
1 green capsicum (bell pepper), sliced
1 stalk celery, chopped
1 bunch bok choy, chopped
400 g (14 oz) canned pineapple pieces in juice

Marinade
45 ml (1 1/2 fl oz) soy sauce
4 teaspoons brown sugar
45 ml (1 1/2 fl oz) dry sherry

Sauce
4 teaspoons corn flour
45 ml (1 1/2 fl oz) soy sauce
45 ml (1 1/2 fl oz) honey
20 ml (2/3 fl oz) brown vinegar
1 pinch ground cinnamon

Place pork in a non-metallic bowl. Combine marinade ingredients and mix through pork. Refrigerate while you prepare the vegetables. Prepare the onion, garlic, red capsicum, green capsicum and celery and place in the slow cooker. Combine sauce ingredients. Add the sauce and the pork and marinade to the slow cooker, stir well and cook on low for 7–9 hours. After 4 hours, add the bok choy. With about 1 hour to go, add the pineapple and juice and stir through. Serve with rice or noodles.

SEAFOOD CASSEROLE

20 ml (2/3 fl oz) olive oil
1 medium onion, roughly chopped
1 leek, finely chopped
2 cloves garlic, crushed
500 ml (approx. 1 pint) canned tomatoes
2 bay leaves
handful chopped fresh parsley
90 ml (3 fl oz) dry white wine
salt and freshly ground black pepper
36 oz (1kg) assorted fish and seafood
handful chopped fresh oregano to garnish

Heat the oil in a frying pan, add onion, leek and garlic and cook for 5 minutes until softened.

Transfer to a slow cooker set on high and add the tomatoes, bay leaves, parsley, wine, salt and pepper. Bring to the simmer, cover and cook for 50 minutes.

Stir in any firm-fleshed fish and cook for 25 minutes. Stir in the soft- fleshed fish, placing the shellfish on the top. Cover with a lid and continue cooking for 40 minutes (until the fish is tender).

Serve garnished with the oregano.

◊ NOTE: Suitable fish and seafood include red mullet, monk fish, sea bream, cod, calamari, mussels, shelled shrimp and clams.

BRAISED FISH WITH LEMON

2 whole bream or pearl perch
salt and freshly ground black pepper
1 tomato, sliced
2 lemons, sliced
olive oil
45 g (1 1/2 oz) butter
fresh parsley leaves to garnish

Remove heads from fish, then scale and clean well. Season cavities with salt and pepper, and place slices of tomato and lemon in each cavity. Grease bowl of a slow cooker with olive oil. Place fish in the slow cooker, side by side, and season with salt and pepper. Top with 2 slices of lemon per fish and a drizzle of olive oil. Cover and cook on low for 1 hour.

Just before serving cut the butter into small cubes and scatter over the top of each piece of fish before covering again. After 10 minutes carefully remove the fish with a large spatula and arrange on a hot serving dish. Pour the remaining liquid from the slow cooker over the fish. Garnish with a scattering of fresh parsley leaves.

BEEF HOTPOT

750 g (1 lb 8 oz) round steak
30 g (1 oz) plain flour
2 teaspoons mustard powder
salt and freshly ground black pepper
1 teaspoon olive oil
1 onion, finely chopped
2 carrots, peeled and grated
2 stalks celery, finely chopped
400 g (14 oz) canned tomatoes
45 ml (1 1/2 fl oz) Worcestershire sauce
2 teaspoons brown sugar, firmly packed
fresh parsley, chopped

Cut steak into 6 serving-size pieces. Coat with mixture of flour, mustard, salt and pepper.

In a large heavy-based frypan, brown meat in oil. Transfer to the slow cooker.

In the same frypan, sauté onion, carrots and celery until glazed. Add tomatoes, Worcestershire sauce and brown sugar. Use the mixture to deglaze the pan then pour juices over meat.

Cover and cook on low for 6–8 hours, or until tender. To serve, spoon sauce over meat and sprinkle with parsley.

BEEF SHORT RIBS

2 kg (4.4 lb) beef short ribs, cut into 5 cm (2 in) lengths
1 onion, chopped
1 teaspoon olive oil
150 ml (5 oz) tomato sauce
60 ml (2 fl oz) soy sauce
60 ml (2 fl oz) apple cider vinegar
30 g (1 oz) brown sugar, firmly packed

Place short ribs on a griller pan and grill until well browned to remove excess fat.

Transfer to the slow cooker. Sauté onion in oil until limp and golden. Add tomato sauce, soy sauce, vinegar and brown sugar and heat until blended. Pour over ribs.

Cover and cook on low for 8 hours.

CURRIED SCALLOPS

250 g (8 oz) scallops
125 ml (4 oz) dry white wine
1 bouquet garni
125 g (4 oz) butter
310 ml (10 oz) cups thin cream
1/2 teaspoon curry powder
salt and freshly ground black pepper
2 egg yolks
45 ml (1 1/2 fl oz) milk

Place scallops, white wine and bouquet garni in the slow cooker and cook on low for approximately 1 hour. Pour off and reserve liquid, discard bouquet garni and keep scallops warm in slow cooker.

Put cooking liquid with butter into a small saucepan and boil hard to reduce. Stir in the cream, curry powder and salt and pepper, and again boil hard for 2–3 minutes. Remove from heat and allow to cool.

Beat egg yolks with milk, and carefully stir into cooled cream mixture. Pour mixture back into slow cooker with the scallops and cook on high for 45–60 minutes. To serve, place a little cooked rice in a small bowl and spoon over 3–4 scallops with a generous quantity of sauce. Serve immediately.

TROUT IN WINE SAUCE

4 trout, cleaned
125 g (4 oz) mushrooms, sliced
125 ml (4 oz) white wine
grated zest and juice of 1 lemon
salt and freshly ground black pepper
125 ml (4 oz) crème fraîche

Grease the slow cooker with a little olive oil and place the trout tail to head in the bottom of the slow cooker.

Add the sliced mushrooms, wine, lemon zest and juice, black pepper and salt. Cover and cook on low for about 3–4 hours.

Stir in the crème fraîche and heat a further 15 minutes.

FISH AND TOMATOES

2 fish fillets (bream or cod)
plain flour
salt and freshly ground black pepper
75 ml (2 1/2 fl oz) vegetable oil
2 onions, peeled and finely chopped
400 g (14 oz) canned chopped tomatoes
20 ml (2/3 fl oz) tablespoon tomato purée
125 ml (4 oz) fish stock
cayenne pepper

Cut the fish to fit into the slow cooker. Season the flour with salt and pepper and coat the fish pieces. Heat the oil in a heavy-based frypan and quickly fry each piece of fish, then place into the slow cooker. Fry the onions until softened and mix in the tomatoes, tomato purée and stock. Bring the sauce to the boil and taste, then season with cayenne. Pour the sauce over the fish and cook on low for 4–6 hours.

HUNTER'S CHICKEN

1 1/2 kg (3 lb 5 oz) chicken pieces
salt and freshly ground black pepper
1 cinnamon stick
2 cloves garlic, chopped
1 green bell pepper (capsicum), chopped
2 small onions, sliced
2 sticks celery, chopped
8 small mushrooms, sliced
90 ml (3 fl oz) cup dry sherry
240 ml (8 fl oz) canned tomatoes, chopped
30 g (1 oz) corn flour
60 ml (2 fl oz) water

Season chicken pieces with salt and pepper. Place the chicken pieces along with all the other ingredients, except corn flour and water, in a slow cooker. Stir well. Cover and cook on high for 3 hours.

Remove chicken pieces and keep warm. Make a smooth paste of corn flour and water and stir into slow cooker. Return chicken, cover and cook for 15 minutes until the gravy thickens. Serve with steamed couscous.

PORK CUTLETS WITH QUINCE

20 ml (2/3 fl oz) olive oil
4 pork cutlets

Sauce

120 ml (4 fl oz) dry white wine
1 clove garlic, crushed
1 medium red onion, sliced
1 medium quince, peeled, cored, cut into thin wedges
juice of 1 orange
90 ml (3 fl oz) chicken stock
1 cinnamon stick
20 ml (2/3 fl oz) honey
chopped fresh parsley, to taste
salt and freshly ground black pepper

Set slow cooker on a high heat setting, add white wine, garlic, onion and quince and cook with the lid on for 20 minutes, stirring occasionally.

Heat oil in a frying pan. Carefully fry pork cutlets on their sides, browning the pork rind only, for 2–3 minutes. Set meat aside.

Stir into slow cooker the orange juice, chicken stock, cinnamon stick and honey. Add the pork and turn down to a low heat setting and cook for 8 hours (or until sauce has thickened slightly). Stir in parsley, salt and pepper, and serve.

CHORIZO AND LENTIL STEW

250 g (9 oz) brown lentils, rinsed
1 L (approx. 2 pints) boiling water
4 tomatoes
875 ml (1 4/5 pints) chicken stock
250 g (9 oz) chorizo sausage, chopped
1 red onion, sliced
2 garlic cloves, crushed
1/2 teaspoon dried crushed chilies
salt and freshly ground black pepper
chopped fresh flat-leaf parsley to garnish

Place the lentils and boiling water in a slow cooker set on high. Cook for 30 minutes, stirring occasionally. Meanwhile, place the tomatoes in a bowl and cover with boiling water. Leave for 30 seconds, then peel, remove the seeds and chop the flesh. Drain the lentils and return to slow cooker with 60 ml (2 fl oz) fresh water and stock.

Put the chorizo into a large heavy-based frying pan and cook over a low heat until the fat starts to run out of the sausage. Increase the heat to high and cook, stirring frequently, for 8 minutes or until browned. Add the onions and cook for 2 more minutes.

Transfer chorizo and onion to the slow cooker, then stir in the chopped tomatoes, garlic and chilies. Season with salt and pepper and cook, covered, for 4 hours, until quite thick but not too dry. Garnish with parsley.

LAMB AND SPINACH CURRY

45 ml (1 1/2 fl oz) vegetable oil
2 onions, chopped
2 cloves garlic, chopped
2 cm (3/4 in) piece fresh root ginger, finely chopped
1 cinnamon stick
1/4 teaspoon ground cloves
3 cardamom pods
750 g (26 1/2 oz) diced lamb
4 teaspoons ground cumin
4 teaspoons ground coriander
90 ml (3 fl oz) natural yoghurt
45 ml (1 1/2 fl oz) tomato paste
180 ml (6 fl oz) beef stock
salt and freshly ground black pepper
100 g (3 oz) baby spinach, chopped
handful of flaked almonds, toasted

Heat the oil in a large heavy-based saucepan. Add onions, garlic, ginger, cinnamon, cloves and cardamom and cook for 5 minutes.

Add the lamb and cook for 5 minutes, turning, until it begins to brown. Transfer to a slow cooker set on high. Mix in the cumin and coriander, then add the yoghurt a quarter at a time, stirring well each time.

Mix together the tomato paste and the stock and add to the lamb. Season to taste. Reduce the heat to low, cover and cook for 7 hours.

Stir in the spinach, cover and simmer for another 15 minutes or until the mixture has reduced slightly. Remove the cinnamon stick and the cardamom pods and mix in the almonds. Serve with rice.

TARRAGON LAMB

60 g (2 oz) butter
1 kg (36 oz) leg of lamb
450 ml (15 oz) chicken stock
165 ml (5 ½ fl oz) dry white wine
1 bunch fresh tarragon
salt and freshly ground black pepper
15 g (1/2 oz) corn flour
20 ml (2/3 fl oz) water
45 ml (1 ½ fl oz) pouring cream

Melt 40 g (1 ½ oz) of the butter in a large heavy-based frying pan over medium heat. Add the lamb and cook for 3 minutes or until browned.

Transfer to a slow cooker on a low setting and add the remaining butter, stock and wine. Cover and cook for 10 hours. Remove the meat and keep warm. Add the tarragon and seasoning to the cooker, turn to high and reduce the liquid by half. Thicken with the corn flour mixed with the water to form a paste, then add the cream. Taste and adjust the seasoning, then remove the tarragon. Slice the lamb and serve with the reduced sauce and roasted vegetables.

OSSO BUCO

45 ml (1 1/2 fl oz) olive oil
36 oz (1kg) veal osso buco
all-purpose (plain) flour for coating veal
1 clove garlic, crushed
1 onion, finely chopped
1 carrot, finely diced
2 sticks celery, finely diced
120 ml (4 fl oz) dry white wine
4 Roma tomatoes, peeled, chopped
150 ml (5 fl oz) cup beef stock
45 ml (1 1/2 fl oz) tomato paste
handful chopped fresh basil
handful chopped fresh parsley
salt and freshly ground black pepper

Heat oil in a large frying pan. Coat osso buco with flour and cook in pan for 3 minutes each side. Remove from the pan and set aside. Add the garlic, onion, carrot and celery to the pan and cook for 5 minutes. Add wine and cook until evaporated. Add the tomatoes, stock and tomato paste to a slow cooker set on low. Add the veal, vegetables and herbs, then season. Cover and simmer for 6 1/2 hours until the meat starts to come away from the bone. Serve with crusty bread.

DRUNKEN BEEF

2 onions, diced
2 carrots, sliced
6 button mushrooms, sliced
165 ml (5 1/2 fl oz) beer
60 ml (2 fl oz) olive oil
450g (15 oz) gravy beef, diced
45 ml (1 1/2 fl oz) tomato paste
salt and freshly ground black pepper
1 teaspoon fresh thyme
1 bay leaf
4 teaspoons all-purpose (plain) flour

In a slow cooker set on high, cook the vegetables in the beer and two thirds of the oil for 10 minutes. Add the meat on top of the vegetables and spoon over the tomato paste. Add the seasoning and herbs. Cook for 1 hour on high then reduce the heat to a low setting.

Add the remaining oil and the flour. Stir to combine all ingredients and cook on a low setting for 8 hours. Remove the bay leaf, taste and adjust the seasoning. Serve with toast, if desired.

FARMER'S CASSEROLE

15 oz (450 g) gravy beef, trimmed of fat, cut into 2 ½ cm (1 in) cubes

2 carrots, diced

2 leeks, sliced

1 onion, diced

240 ml (8 fl oz) beef stock

salt and freshly ground black pepper

400 (14 oz) canned butter beans, rinsed, drained

45 g (1 1/2 oz) frozen peas

Cheese Dumplings

100 g (3 1/2 oz) self-rising (self-raising) flour

1 teaspoon finely chopped fresh parsley

45 g (1 1/2 oz) Cheddar cheese, grated

45 g (1 1/2 oz) butter, cut into small cubes

45 ml (1 1/2 fl oz) water

Place the meat and the vegetables in a slow cooker set on a high setting. Stir in the stock and season well. Cover and cook for 3 1/2 hours.

Meanwhile, make the dumplings by combining all the dry ingredients in a bowl. Using your fingertips, rub in the butter and water to form a soft dough. Shape the dough into 12 equal dumplings.

Preheat the oven to 350°F (180°C).

Stir the butter beans and peas into the casserole, and season. Arrange dumplings over the top and put the uncovered dish in the oven for 30 minutes or until the dumplings are golden.

◊ NOTE: This recipe requires you to finish the dumplings in the oven so you will need to use a slow cooker with a cooking dish that can be removed from the electrical component and safely put into the oven.

MAINS

BOUILLABAISE

1 1/2 kg (3 lb, 5 oz) mixed fish and seafood, including firm white fish fillets, shrimp (prawn), mussels, crab and calamari rings

60 ml (2 fl oz) cup olive oil

2 cloves garlic, crushed

2 large onions, chopped

2 leeks, sliced

2 x 400 g (14 oz) cans of tomatoes

165 ml (5 1/2 fl oz) fish stock

4 teaspoons chopped fresh thyme or 1 teaspoon dried thyme

8 teaspoons chopped fresh basil or 1 1/2 teaspoons dried basil

8 teaspoons chopped fresh parsley

2 bay leaves

8 teaspoons finely grated orange rind

1 teaspoon saffron threads

165 ml (5 1/2 fl oz) dry white wine

freshly ground black pepper

Remove the bones and skin from the fish fillets and cut into 2 cm (3/4 in) cubes. Peel and devein the prawns, leaving the tails intact. Scrub and remove the beards from the mussels. Cut the crab into quarters. Set aside.

Heat a slow cooker on a high setting, then add the oil, garlic, onions, leeks, tomatoes and stock and cook for 1 1/2 hours. Add the thyme, basil, parsley, bay leaves, orange rind, saffron and wine. Cook for 30 minutes.

Add the fish and crab and cook for 1 hour. Add the remaining seafood and cook for 1 hour longer or until all fish and seafood are cooked. Season to taste with black pepper.

FISH AND COCONUT CURRY

2 tomatoes
2 cardamom pods, bruised
1 teaspoon ground coriander
1 teaspoon ground cumin
1 teaspoon ground cinnamon
1 teaspoon hot chili powder
1/2 teaspoon ground turmeric
45 ml (1 1/2 fl oz) water
45 ml (1 1/2 fl oz) vegetable oil
1 onion, finely chopped
1 clove garlic, finely chopped
2.5 cm (1 in) piece fresh root ginger, finely chopped
400 ml (14 oz) coconut milk
700 g (24 oz) skinless white fish fillet, such as haddock or cod, cut into 1 in (25 mm) chunks
salt to taste
fresh cilantro (coriander) leaves to garnish

Place tomatoes in a bowl, cover with boiling water and leave to stand for 30 seconds. Peel, then finely chop. Crush cardamom seeds using a mortar and pestle. Add coriander, cumin, cinnamon, chili powder, turmeric and water and mix to a paste. Set aside.

Heat oil in a large heavy-based saucepan. Cook onion, garlic and ginger for 3 minutes or until softened. Add spice paste, mix well and cook for 1 minute, stirring constantly.

Transfer to a slow cooker on a high setting, pour in coconut milk and bring to the simmer for 30 minutes. Add fish, tomatoes and salt. Partly cover and cook for a further 45 minutes or until fish turns opaque and is cooked through. Garnish with cilantro leaves and serve on a bed of rice.

PAELLA

20 ml (2/3 fl oz) olive oil

2 onions, chopped

2 cloves garlic, crushed

handful fresh thyme leaves

2 teaspoons finely grated lemon rind

4 ripe tomatoes, chopped

525 g (18 1/2 oz) short-grain white rice

pinch saffron threads, soaked in 500 ml (1 pint) water

1 1/4 L (2 1/2 pints) chicken or fish stock

300 g (10 oz) fresh or frozen peas

2 red capsicums (bell peppers), chopped

1 kg (36 oz) mussels, scrubbed, de-bearded

500 g (17 1/2 oz) firm white fish fillets, chopped

300 g (10 oz) peeled uncooked shrimp (prawns)

200 g (7 oz) scallops

3 calamari, cleaned, sliced

4 teaspoons chopped fresh parsley

Preheat slow cooker to a high heat level. Add the oil and the onions and stir, then add the garlic, thyme, lemon rind and tomatoes and cook for 15 minutes.

Add the rice and saffron mixture and warmed stock. Simmer, stirring occasionally, for 1 1/2 hours or until the rice has absorbed almost all the liquid.

Stir in the peas, peppers and mussels and cook for 20 minutes. Add the fish, shrimp and scallops and cook for 20 minutes. Stir in the calamari and parsley and cook for 20 minutes longer or until the seafood is cooked.

CHICKEN WITH CHORIZO

8 chicken drumsticks
2 tablespoons olive oil
1 onion, sliced
2 cloves garlic, crushed
1 red capsicum (bell pepper), sliced
1 yellow capsicum (bell pepper), sliced
2 teaspoons paprika
60 ml (2 fl oz) dry sherry or dry vermouth
500 ml (17 fl oz) canned chopped tomatoes
1 bay leaf
1 strip orange rind
2 chorizo sausages, sliced
large handful pitted black olives
salt and freshly ground black pepper

Place the chicken in a large non-stick frying pan and cook without oil for 12 minutes, turning occasionally, until golden. Remove the chicken and set aside. Drain any fat from the pan and discard.

Add the oil to the pan and cook the onion, garlic and peppers for 3 minutes, until softened. Transfer the mixture to a slow cooker set on low, add the chicken and the paprika, sherry or vermouth, tomatoes, bay leaf and orange rind. Bring to temperature and cook for 5 hours.

Add the chorizo and olives and cook for a further 30 minutes, then season.

◊   NOTE: Packed with Mediterranean taste, this casserole is equally good with rice or crusty bread. You can use stock or orange juice instead of the sherry or vermouth.

CHICKEN CASSEROLE

45 ml (1 1/2 fl oz) oil
8 chicken drumsticks
salt and freshly ground black pepper
4 onions, sliced
10 1/2 oz (300ml) chicken stock
1/2 teaspoon chili powder
8 teaspoons all-purpose (plain) flour
2 x 400 g (14 oz) canned tomatoes
1 x 400 g (14 oz) canned red kidney beans, rinsed, drained
45 g (1 ½ oz) butter

Heat the oil in a large frying pan over medium heat. Add the chicken, season and cook until browned. Add the onions and fry for 1 minute.

Heat stock in a small saucepan until simmering. In a preheated slow cooker set on high, sprinkle the chilli powder and flour. Slowly add the stock, stirring constantly. Transfer chicken and onions to slow cooker and add the tomatoes, beans and butter. Cover and cook for 3 1/2 hours on high.

JUGGED CHICKEN

60 g (2 oz) butter
8 small onions, peeled
1 1/2 kg (3 lb 5 oz) whole chicken
3 tomatoes, cut into wedges
100 g (3 1/2 oz) smoked ham or bacon, diced
2 bay leaves
2 cloves garlic, crushed
2 teaspoons Dijon mustard
180 ml (6 fl oz) dry white wine
60 ml (3 fl oz) port wine
45 ml (1 1/2 fl oz) brandy
salt and freshly ground black pepper

Melt 20 g (2/3 oz) butter in a large heavy- based frying pan over medium heat. Add onions and cook for 2 minutes, stirring constantly. Brush chicken all over with the remaining butter. Add chicken to pan and cook for 4 minutes.

In a slow cooker set on low, arrange tomatoes, ham or bacon and bay leaves over base of dish. Add the contents of the frying pan and splash the pan with a little of the white wine and add to the slow cooker as well.

3. Blend together garlic, mustard, remaining white wine, port wine, brandy, salt and pepper. Pour over chicken, cover and cook for 7 hours.

◊   NOTE: As an alternative you can carefully remove the ceramic insert with the jugged chicken in the last 15 minutes of cooking and put in an oven, preheated to 400°F (200°C). Bake with the lid removed to brown the chicken. Cut the chicken into pieces and serve with crispy potatoes and salad.

SWEET AND SPICY CHICKEN WINGS

45 ml (1 1/2 fl oz) vegetable oil
1 kg (36 oz) chicken wings
1 large onion, finely chopped
1 clove garlic, crushed
1 1/2 teaspoons grated fresh ginger
1/2 teaspoon ground turmeric
1/2 teaspoon ground cumin
1 cinnamon stick
60 ml (2 fl oz) cider vinegar
500 ml (17 fl oz) apricot nectar
salt and freshly ground black pepper
90 g (3 oz) dried prunes, pitted
90 g (3 oz) dried apricots
4 teaspoons honey
60 ml lemon juice

Heat the oil in a large saucepan. Add the chicken wings, a few at a time, and brown lightly on both sides. Remove to a plate as they brown.

Add onion and cook for 2 minutes. Stir in the garlic and cook for a further minute, then transfer mix to a slow cooker set to low. Add the chicken, ginger and spices. Stir and turn the wings to coat. Add the vinegar and apricot nectar and season to taste. Cover and cook for 6 hours.

Add the prunes, apricots, honey and lemon juice. Cover and simmer for 2 more hours and then remove lid, turn to high and simmer for 35 minutes. If a thicker sauce is desired, remove the wings and fruit to a serving platter and simmer until the sauce reduces. Pour the sauce over the wings and Serve with steamed couscous or rice, garnished with a sprig of parsley.

PORK SPARE RIBS

750 g (26 1/2 oz) pork spare ribs
30 ml (1 fl oz) peanut oil
1 teaspoon ground coriander
1/2 teaspoon ground cumin
1/2 teaspoon freshly ground black pepper
45 ml (1 1/2 fl oz) soy sauce
4 teaspoons tamarind concentrate
1 teaspoon brown sugar
60 ml (2 fl oz) water

Paste
2 French shallots, chopped
2 cloves garlic
2 teaspoons finely grated fresh ginger
60 ml (2 fl oz) water

Pound the paste ingredients in a mortar and pestle or combine in a small food processor. Chop spare ribs in half. Heat 20 ml (2/3 fl oz) oil in a wok or medium frying pan. Add spare ribs in 2 batches and fry for 2–3 minutes or until ribs are golden and crisp. Remove and set aside.

Heat remaining oil and add paste. Cook for 2 minutes, stirring constantly. Add coriander, cumin, black pepper, soy sauce, tamarind and sugar.

Turn all ingredients out into slow cooker set on a high heat setting. Return ribs to sauce, add water and cook for 4 hours, basting and turning every hour. Add a little extra water if sauce becomes too thick. Serve with Chinese greens and a side bowl of rice.

PORK MEATBALLS

180 g (6 oz) white breadcrumbs
240 ml (8 fl oz) buttermilk
500 g (17 1/2 oz) lean pork mince
250 g (9 oz) lean beef mince
2 eggs
1 medium onion, finely chopped
2 teaspoons salt
3/4 teaspoon dill seeds
1/4 teaspoon allspice
1/8 teaspoon ground nutmeg
60 g (2 oz) butter
250 ml (8 1/2 fl oz) chicken stock
120 ml (4 fl oz) dry white wine
freshly ground black pepper
240 ml (8 fl oz) cream
handful fresh parsley leaves to garnish

Soak breadcrumbs in buttermilk for 5 minutes. Add meats, eggs, onion, salt, herbs and spices. Mix well, cover and refrigerate for 30 minutes.

Shape tablespoon quantities of mixture into balls. Heat butter in a medium frying pan and cook meatballs until lightly browned.

Place meatballs into the slow cooker as they are browned. Add stock, wine and pepper. Cover and cook on low for 5 hours. Approximately 20 minutes before serving turn the heat to high and add cream. Serve meatballs garnished with parsley and accompanied by crusty bread.

◊ TIP: The meatballs will have a finer texture if the meats are minced together twice (ask your butcher to do this).

TUSCAN SAUSAGE POT

45 ml (1 1/2 fl oz) olive oil
500 g (17 1/2 oz) pork sausages
1 red onion, sliced
2 sticks celery, sliced
1 large carrot, diced
1 clove garlic, crushed
4 Roma tomatoes
120 ml (4 fl oz) dry white wine
salt and freshly ground black pepper
400 g (14 oz) canned cannellini beans, rinsed
1 L (approx. 2 pints) water
1 teaspoon salt
200 g (7 oz) instant polenta
30 g (1 oz) butter
chopped fresh flat-leaf parsley to garnish

Heat 4 teaspoons of the oil in a large frying pan and cook
the sausages for 5 minutes or until browned, turning
occasionally. Remove from the pan. Add the remaining oil
and cook the onion, celery, carrot and garlic for 3–4 minutes,
until lightly colored.

Put the tomatoes in a bowl and cover with boiling water.
Leave for 30 seconds, then peel and quarter.

Place the tomatoes, sausages and sautéed vegetables into a
slow cooker set on high and add the wine and the seasoning.
Cook for 2 hours.

Add the beans and cook for a further 1 1/2 hours. Just before
the sausage pot is ready bring water to the boil in a large
saucepan and add salt. Sprinkle in the polenta and stir for 5
minutes or until thick and smooth, then add the butter. Serve
with the sausage pot, sprinkled with parsley.

PORK WITH CUMIN

3 cloves garlic, crushed
1 teaspoon ground cumin
finely grated rind of 1 lemon
45 ml (1 1/2 fl oz) lemon juice
2 teaspoons Dijon mustard
120 ml (4 fl oz) dry white wine
large handful chopped fresh cilantro (coriander)
750 g (17 oz) fillet pork, cut into 2 cm (3/4 in) pieces
60 ml (2 fl oz) olive oil
1 onion, sliced
180 ml (6 fl oz) chicken stock
salt and freshly ground black pepper
cilantro (coriander) leaves to garnish

Mix together garlic, cumin, lemon rind, lemon juice, mustard, white wine and cilantro in a shallow bowl. Add pork and coat well in the mixture.

Heat 2/3 of the oil in a large frying pan over medium to high heat. Remove pork from marinade with a slotted spoon, reserving marinade. Add pork to frying pan and cook in batches until golden. Remove and set aside. Heat remaining oil and cook onion until soft.

Place pork and onion in a slow cooker set on low and add the remaining marinade and chicken stock. Cover and simmer for 4 1/2 hours. Season with salt and pepper and garnish with cilantro leaves. Serve pork with lemon wedges and fried potatoes.

BOBOTIE

1 tablespoon vegetable oil

1 onion, finely chopped

2 thick slices of white bread, broken into pieces (crusts removed)

300 ml (10 fl oz) milk

500 g (17 oz) lean lamb mince

8 teaspoons curry paste

2 cloves garlic, crushed

salt and freshly ground black pepper

juice of 1/2 lemon

50 g (1 3/4 oz) dried apricots, chopped

50 g (1 3/4 oz) raisins

60 g (2 oz) flaked almonds

2 eggs

Heat the oil in a large heavy-based frying pan, add the onion and fry for 5 minutes to soften. Place the bread in a bowl with the milk and leave to soak.

Meanwhile, add the lamb to the pan and cook for 10 minutes or until browned, breaking it up with a wooden spoon. Transfer the lamb to a slow cooker set on high and add the curry paste, garlic and seasoning and cook for 30 minutes. Add the lemon juice, apricots and raisins and half of the almonds and mix well.

Lift the bread out of the milk and squeeze gently to remove some of the liquid. Reserve the milk and add the bread to the slow cooker. Cover and cook for 2 hours.

Preheat the oven to 350°F (180°C). Whisk the eggs into the remaining milk and season. Pour over the lamb mixture and sprinkle with the remaining almonds. Transfer the ovenproof part of the slow cooker to the oven and cook for 30 minutes or until the top has set and is golden.

MEATBALLS WITH EGG AND LEMON SAUCE

375 ml (15 fl oz) beef stock

500 g (17 oz) lean lamb mince

1 small onion, chopped

5 egg yolks

1 teaspoon chopped fresh mint

1 teaspoon chopped fresh oregano

4 teaspoons chopped fresh parsley

salt and freshly ground black pepper

8 teaspoons rice

juice of 1 lemon

Place 240 ml (8 fl oz) of stock in a slow cooker on high. Cover and heat. Combine lamb, onion, 1 egg yolk, mint, oregano and parsley in a large bowl. Season with salt and pepper and add remaining stock. Roll tablespoon quantities into balls, then roll lightly in rice.

Transfer meatballs into slow cooker. Cover, turn to low and cook for 6 hours. In a medium-sized bowl beat remaining egg yolks, slowly adding lemon juice until combined. Slowly add most of the hot stock from slow cooker, beating constantly until well combined and mixture thickens. Stir over low heat in a small saucepan if necessary. Serve the sauce drizzled over the meatballs.

CHILI BEEF

4 thin-cut beef sirloin steaks
4 strips rindless bacon, finely chopped
4 teaspoons chopped fresh parsley
1/2 teaspoon dried marjoram
60 g (2 oz) fresh breadcrumbs
60 g (2 oz) all-purpose (plain) flour
salt and freshly ground black pepper
toothpicks
20 ml (2/3 fl oz) olive oil
1 teaspoon chili powder
1 onion, diced
2 cloves garlic, crushed
1 red bell pepper (capsicum), diced
240 ml (8 fl oz) beef stock
2 x 400 g (14 oz) cans red kidney beans, rinsed, drained

Place the beef between sheets of non-stick baking paper
and flatten. Heat a large frying pan over medium heat. Add
bacon and cook for 3 minutes, draining off any excess fat.
Remove from the heat and mix with the parsley, marjoram
and breadcrumbs. Combine the flour, salt and pepper in a
shallow dish. Divide the bacon mixture between slices of
the beef, then roll up each slice from the short end, turn it in
the seasoned flour and secure it with a toothpick. Heat the
oil in a large frying pan over medium heat, add the beef and
cook for 2 minutes, turning, until browned. Remove from pan
and place in a slow cooker set on low. Add the chili powder,
onion, garlic and bell pepper. Gently pour over the stock.
Cover the dish then cook for 6 hours. Add the kidney beans
and cook for another 3 hours. Remove the cocktail sticks to
serve.

GREEN CHICKEN CURRY

1 kg (2.2 lb) chicken breast, diced
45 ml (1 1/2 fl oz) olive oil
90 ml (3 fl oz) green curry paste
400 ml (13 oz) coconut milk
100 g (3 1/2 oz) green beans, chopped
100 g (3 1/2 oz) cauliflower, chopped
1 red capsicum (bell pepper), chopped
2 teaspoons sugar

In a heavy-based frypan, heat the olive oil and brown the chicken. Place all ingredients including the chicken into the slow cooker and combine. Cover and cook on high for 6–7 hours or low for 8–10 hours. Serve with steamed jasmine rice.

JAMBALAYA

500 g (18 oz) boneless chicken breasts, cut into 25 mm (1 in) cubes

300 g (10 1/2 oz) smoked sausage, sliced

1/2 onion, chopped

1 green capsicum (bell pepper), chopped

800 g (1 lb 10 oz) canned crushed tomatoes

250 ml (8 oz) chicken stock

125 ml (4 oz) dry white wine

2 teaspoons dried oregano

2 teaspoons dried parsley flakes

2 teaspoons Cajun seasoning

1 teaspoon cayenne pepper

500 g (18 oz) cooked prawns (shrimp)

400 g (14 oz) white rice, cooked

Combine chicken, sausage, onion, and capsicum in slow cooker. Add tomatoes, chicken stock, wine, oregano, parsley, Cajun seasoning and pepper and stir gently. Cover and cook on low for 6–8 hours or on high for 3–4 hours.

About 30–45 minutes before eating, add cooked prawns and hot cooked rice. Heat thoroughly before serving.

DESSERTS

APRICOT MOUSSE

250 g (8 oz) dried apricots
2 floury cooking apples, peeled and thinly sliced
juice and zest of 1 lemon
60 g (2 oz) raw sugar
3 egg whites
125 ml (4 oz) thickened cream, whipped

Soak dried apricots for approximately 1 hour, then drain well. Place into slow cooker with apples, lemon juice and zest and sugar. Cook on low for 3–4 hours or on high for 2–3 hours, until apricots are soft and apples cooked. Drain fruit, discarding liquid, and purée in a blender or food processor. Chill.

Beat egg whites until stiff. Beat the cream in a separate bowl, then fold half the cream into the egg whites. Carefully fold egg white mixture and remaining cream through the fruit purée. Chill.

HOT CARAMEL MERINGUE DESSERT

60 g raw sugar

375 ml (12 oz) evaporated milk

1 teaspoon vanilla extract

3 thick slices wholemeal bread, crusts removed, cubed

50 g (1 2/3 oz) sultanas (golden raisins)

50 g (1 2/3 oz) cup raisins, chopped

zest of 1 orange, grated

3 eggs, separated

60 ml (2 oz) thin cream

1 teaspoon lemon juice

75 g (2 1/2 oz) caster sugar

1 teaspoon dried coconut

Dissolve sugar in a heavy-based saucepan over low heat. Once melted, increase heat and allow to cook without stirring until a deep golden brown. Remove from heat.

Bring the milk to the boil. Slowly pour hot milk into the hot toffee, stirring to form a smooth caramel. Add vanilla.

Mix together bread cubes, dried fruits and orange zest. Add caramel and allow to stand for about half an hour.

Beat egg yolks and cream, and add lemon juice. Stir gently into cooling caramel mixture. Allow to cool, then pour into an ovenproof basin, cover with foil and tie firmly with kitchen string. Fill the slow cooker with about 5 cm (2 in) of water and put in the basin. Cook on low for 2 1/2–3 hours. Remove, take off foil covering and allow to cool.

Preheat oven to 200°C (400°F). Whip the egg whites, gradually adding the sugar, then swirl on top of cooled pudding and sprinkle with coconut. Place in oven and cook for 15–20 minutes or until meringue is golden and crisp.

GRAND MARNIER CRÉME CARAMEL

100 g (3 1/2 oz) white sugar
3 eggs
625 ml (1 pint 4 oz) milk
30 ml (1 oz) Grand Marnier

Melt half the sugar slowly in a heavy saucepan. Do not stir, just allow to melt into toffee.

Butter 4 small heatproof crème caramel molds, then pour the melted sugar quickly into base of dishes and swirl around the sides as high as possible.

Beat eggs well and whisk into milk with Grand Marnier and the remaining sugar. Keep whisking until sugar has dissolved, then pour mixture into caramel molds and cover with foil. Place molds into slow cooker and pour sufficient cold water around the bases to come halfway up the sides. Cook on low for approximately 3–4 hours.

Remove crème caramels from slow cooker and chill thoroughly. Serve either in the molds or very carefully turned out onto plates, with any caramel left behind spooned over the top.

RIPE FRUIT COMPOTE

6 apricots, halved and stoned
150 g (5 oz) cherries
6 fresh plums
1 apple, sliced
100 g (3 ½ oz) sugar
rind of 1 orange
3 cloves

Combine all ingredients in the slow cooker and cook on low
for 2–3 hours or on high for 1–1 1/2 hours. Remove cloves
and orange rind and test for sweetness, adding sugar or
honey to taste.

Allow to cool, then serve with cream. This is a marvelous
recipe for using up overripe fruit.

SPICED PEACHES

handful of cloves
600 g (21 oz) canned peach halves, with juice
1 cinnamon stick
30 ml (1 oz) brandy, orange liqueur or orange juice

Press 5 cloves into each peach half and arrange halves in
the base of the slow cooker.

Combine peach juice and brandy, liqueur or orange juice, add
the cinnamon stick and pour mixture over peaches.
Cook on low for 2–3 hours or on high for 1–1 1/2 hours.
Serve hot or chilled, with cream.

The peaches will keep in the refrigerator for at least a week.

MARMALADE PUDDING

500 ml (1 pint) milk
120 g (4 oz) fresh, fine breadcrumbs
3 eggs, separated
60 g (2 oz) caster (super fine) sugar
30 ml (1 oz) dark marmalade

Bring milk to the boil and pour over breadcrumbs. Allow to cool. Beat the egg yolks with the sugar, then add the marmalade. Stir into the cold bread and milk mixture. Beat the egg whites until stiff and fold in. Grease a pudding basin and lightly spoon in the pudding mixture.

Cover basin tightly with foil and tie with kitchen string, forming a loop at the top so that the basin may be easily removed from the slow cooker. Place basin into cooker, pour over boiling water and cook on high for about 3 hours.

Remove basin, carefully turn out pudding and serve with hot custard.

BAKED BREAD AND BUTTER PUDDING

4 thin slices stale brown or white bread, buttered

75 g (2 1/2 oz) mixed sultanas (golden raisins) and currants

50 g (1 2/3 oz) raw sugar

1/2 teaspoon grated nutmeg or cinnamon

2 eggs

625 ml (1 pint 4 oz) milk

1 teaspoon vanilla extract

zest of 1/2 orange, grated

Remove crusts from bread and cut into thick fingers. Grease an ovenproof dish and arrange bread in layers, buttered-side up. Sprinkle layers with dried fruit, sugar and spice.

Beat together eggs, milk and vanilla and stir in orange zest. Pour mixture over layered bread and allow to stand for approximately 30 minutes. Cover dish with lid or foil.

Pour 250 ml (8 oz) hot water into the slow cooker, then insert the pudding dish and cook on high for 3–4 hours.

BANANAS IN RUM AND HONEY SYRUP

6 firm bananas, peeled
30 ml (1 oz) dark rum
15 ml (1/2 oz) honey
30 ml (1 oz) orange juice
juice of 1/2 lemon
1/2 teaspoon ground cinnamon

Arrange bananas in base of slow cooker. Combine rum, honey, juices and cinnamon and spoon over and around bananas. Cook on high for approximately 1/2–3/4 hour or on low for approximately 1 hour, until bananas are just tender and syrup is heated through.

Serve bananas with scoops of ice cream, with syrup spooned over.

LEMON SAGO PUDDING

200 g (7 oz) uncooked sago
1 large egg
250 ml (8 oz) milk
1–2 tablespoons raw sugar
1 teaspoon vanilla extract
1/2 teaspoon ground nutmeg
zest of 1 lemon, grated

Bring 250 ml (8 1/2 fl oz) cup water to a fast boil and pour in the sago. Cook at a quick simmer, stirring often, until sago is translucent (about 15 minutes). If the water is absorbed before the sago is cooked, add a little more. When done, pour the sago into a bowl and allow to cool.

Beat together the egg, milk and sugar in a bowl, then add remaining ingredients and sago. Pour mixture into a lightly greased dish, sprinkle with extra nutmeg and cover with a lid or foil.

INDEX

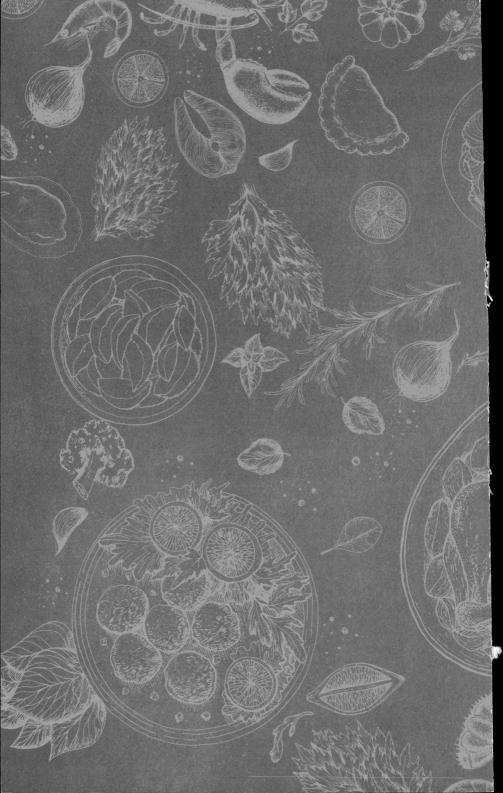